Stocking Stuffers: Christmas Joke Book for Kids, Teens, Adults & Seniors

Unwrap Laughter with 400+ Funny Puns, Riddles, and One-Liners—A Festive Gift for the Whole Family to Share Holiday Cheer

Whimsy Works Wonders

Contents

Santa's Silly Sled

Ho Ho Ho! Welcome to Santa's Silly Sled, the most magical sleigh ride you'll ever take! Here in Santa's special joke section, we've packed in enough laughs to keep you smiling from the North Pole to your living room.

Get ready to meet mischievous elves, dancing reindeer, and even a few snowmen with their own funny twist! These jokes are perfect for sharing with your friends, telling at the dinner table, or making your family burst out laughing by the Christmas tree.

Whether you're imagining Santa trying to wrap a giant present or picturing Rudolph getting up to some reindeer hijinks, there's something here to make everyone smile.

Remember, Santa's sled only runs on holiday cheer—and that means plenty of laughs! So, grab your jingle bells, cozy up with your family, and let's get ready to fill this holiday season with endless fun.

Laughter is the best gift of all, and Santa's got plenty to share.

Let's get sledding and let the giggles begin!

How to Redeem Your Digital Bonuses

1) **Scan the QR Code**: Find the QR code below this paragraph. Using your smartphone or tablet, open the camera app and point it at the code. A message or link will appear—tap the link, and you'll land on a page with two options: **leave a review** or **claim your bonuses**.

2) **Enter Your Email**: If you'd like, you can **leave a review** to share your thoughts about the book before claiming your bonuses.

Afterward, Click "**Claim Your Bonuses**," and you'll be taken to a simple page to enter your email. Rest assured, your email will only be used for book-related updates.

3) **Check Your Email**: After entering your email, check your inbox. If the email doesn't appear, don't forget to check your ***spam or promotions folder***.

Funny Puns for Santa's Silly Sled

Why did Santa's helper see the doctor?
He had low "elf-esteem!"

What do snowmen eat for breakfast?
Frosted Flakes, of course!

Why did Rudolph bring an umbrella to the Christmas party? Because he heard it was going to "reindeer!"

How does Santa stay cool during the summer?
He likes to chill with his "ice elf-cream!"

Why did the Christmas tree get in trouble?
Because it couldn't stop "branching" out!

What do reindeer say when they tell jokes to each other?
They say, "This one will sleigh you!"

Why did the reindeer sign up for comedy?
He wanted to learn how to "sleigh" an audience!

Why did Santa use GPS?
To make sure he wasn't lost in a "winter wonderland!"

Elves and Santa's Helpers Jokes

What's an elf's favorite kind of music?
"Wrap" music—it really gets them in the gift-giving groove!

Why did the elf get kicked out of Santa's workshop?
He was always "elf-ing" around and never got any work done!

Why did the elf get promoted?
Because he had plenty of "elf-confidence!"

What did the elf say to the Christmas bell?
"Stop ringing my ears!"

What did Santa say to the nervous elf?
"Don't worry, I've got it 'claused' and handled!"

Why did the elf put his bed in the fireplace?
Because he wanted to sleep like a "log!"

What's an elf's favorite kind of salad?
"Iceberg lettuce"—it's always the coolest!

Animals and Playful Adventures Jokes

Why did the chicken join the band?
Because it had the best drumsticks!

What do you get if you cross a snowman with a dog?
Frostbite!

Why did the squirrel bring a ladder to the tree?
To reach the "nut"-thing up top!

Why did the cat sit on the computer?
It wanted to keep an eye on the mouse!

Why did the cow love playing hide and seek?
Because it always "moo-ved" quietly!

Why don't fish do well in school?
Because they're swimming through their homework!

Why did the horse never get lost?
Because he always followed his "neigh-vigation" system.

How do you make a tissue dance?
You put a little "boogie" in it!

Kids Life and General Jokes

Why was the math book always stressed out?
It had too many "problems."

Why don't students tell secrets in a garden?
Because the potatoes have "eyes!"

Why did the student eat his homework?
The teacher said it was a piece of "cake."

Why did the teddy bear say no to dessert?
Because it was already stuffed!

Why did the pencil look worried?
Because it was running out of "points."

What did the crayon say to the coloring book?
"You bring out the best in me!"

Why did the kid take a ladder to school?
He wanted to go to "high" school!

Why did the glue cross the playground?
To stick to the other side!

Riddles for Santa's Silly Sled

I come with many colors, so bright and so bold, I turn houses festive when it gets cold. What am I?
Christmas lights!

I'm full of branches but I don't grow leaves,
I often hold memories of families' holiday eves.
What am I?
A Christmas tree!

I hang around all year waiting for Christmas, and you fill me up with treats. What am I?
A Christmas stocking!

I light up the room with warmth and cheer, and when you blow me out, I disappear. What am I?
A candle!

I help count the days until Christmas arrives, every day you open a door for a surprise. What am I?
An advent calendar!

Riddles for Santa's Silly Sled

It's time to put on your thinking caps, kids! Santa's elves have come up with some of the trickiest, silliest riddles to keep you guessing. These aren't just any riddles—they're full of Christmas magic, designed to make you laugh while you solve them! Gather your family, challenge your friends, and see who can answer these riddles the fastest.

Get ready to giggle, scratch your head, and maybe even shout 'Aha!' when you find the answer. Are you ready to riddle your way through the holiday cheer? Let's get started!

Winter Riddles

I get tossed around but I never get mad, I make a big splash, and the kids are glad. What am I?

A snowball!

What falls but never gets hurt?

Snow!

What has four legs, barks, and loves rolling in the snow but never melts?

A snow-dog!

I'm made of buttons, coal, and a hat, I stand outside, but I'm not a bat. What am I?

A snowman!

What kind of bread does Frosty the Snowman eat?

Chill-abatta!

What does Frosty use to call his friends?

A snow-phone!

What do you call a snowman on rollerblades?

A snowmobile!

Holiday Treats and Festive Fun Riddles

I have a jolly laugh, a fluffy red suit, and I fly through the air to deliver the loot. Who am I?

Santa Claus!

I fly through the night without a sound, delivering gifts while I'm magic-bound. Who am I?

Santa's sleigh!

I bring gifts and joy, but I never leave any footprints. Who am I?

An elf!

What's red, white, and pepperminty, hanging on a tree until someone gets hungry?

A candy cane!

I work around the clock to make sure every gift is perfectly wrapped, but I'm not Santa. Who am I?

An elf!

What jingles all the way but isn't a bell?

Santa's sleigh!

Kids Play, Toys, and Animals Riddles

I have wheels and a bell, and when you pedal, I move really well. What am I?

A bicycle!

I am small, furry, and often a child's best friend, I squeak when I'm happy and love to spin.

What am I?

A hamster!

I have four legs and go "woof," I love running and playing, and I'm your fluffy goof. Who am I?

A dog!

I'm stuffed and cuddly, and I keep you safe at night.

What am I?

A teddy bear!

I come in many colors, and you stack me high, you build towers and castles before waving goodbye.

What am I?

Building blocks!

Kids Play, Toys, and Animals Riddles

I'm full of pages, full of colors, full of fun, grab some crayons, and let's make art when we're done.

What am I?

A coloring book!

I have a mane, four legs, and a tail, and when you rock back and forth, I make you smile.

What am I?

A rocking horse!

I am a toy that hops on its spring, kids love to bounce, and I love to swing. What am I?

A pogo stick!

I have buttons and a screen, and I make cool beeps; you can play all day until it's time for sleep.

What am I?

A handheld video game!

I love to bounce, and you throw me around, catch me, and I come back without making a sound.

What am I?

A rubber ball!

One-Liners for Santa's Silly Sled

Get ready for a burst of quick laughs! These one-liners are short, sweet, and perfect for making everyone giggle in a flash. Whether you're sharing them around the dinner table, at a holiday party, or just trying to make someone smile, these jokes are sure to deliver a festive dose of fun.

Let's dive into these snappy jokes and keep the holiday cheer going strong!

Technology and School Jokes

The computer broke up with the printer it just didn't have a "connection"!

The kid brought a ladder to school to get to "high" school!

Your nose can't be 12 inches long—
then it would be a "foot"!

The notebook went to the dance to
"take notes" on all the moves!

The computer was cold because it left its "Windows" open!

The music teacher needed a ladder to reach the
"high notes"!

The math book looked sad—it had too many "problems"!

The pencil got a timeout because it couldn't "stay on point"!

The marker felt popular because it always "drew" attention!

A bear stuck in the rain is a "drizzly bear"!

The bicycle fell over—it was "two-tired"!

A pig who knows karate is called a "pork chop"!

17

Technology and School Jokes

The teddy bear couldn't finish dessert—it was already "stuffed"!

The frog took the bus—his car got "toad"!

To catch a squirrel, just climb a tree and act like a "nut"!

A sleeping dinosaur is a "dino-snore"!

The scarecrow won an award because he was outstanding in his field!

Fish are smart because they live in schools!

The bee got married because he found his "honey"!

A dog magician is called a "labra-cadabra-dor"!

The owl had friends over to have a real "hoot"!

Seagulls fly over the sea; otherwise, they'd be called "bagels"!

Food Jokes

The cookie went to the doctor—it felt "crummy"!

What do you call cheese that isn't yours?
"Nacho" cheese!

What kind of key opens a banana? A "monkey"!

The grape stopped in the road—it ran out of juice!

The hotdog said, "I'm on a roll!"

The apple stopped hanging out with the orange—
it got "bruised"!

The golfer brought two pairs of pants—
in case he got a "hole in one"!

Ghosts are bad at lying—they're too "transparent"!
Ninjas wear "sneakers"!

The kid crossed the playground to get to the other slide!

The ocean said nothing to the shore—it just waved!

Family Stories for a Festive Christmas Eve

There's nothing quite like gathering around with family during the holidays, sharing laughter, and making memories that will last for years to come.

This collection of funny, heartwarming stories is perfect for just that—especially on a Christmas Eve when everyone's bundled up, sipping hot cocoa, and waiting for Santa.

These stories are filled with moments of mischief, innocent misunderstandings, and the delightful chaos that comes with being a kid. Whether it's wrapping Santa in foil, discovering Mrs. Claus at the dinner table, or chasing a runaway hamster, each story is meant to be read aloud, bringing joy to kids and adults alike.

So settle in, gather your loved ones, and get ready to laugh together as we take a festive dive into these funny holiday tales.

Let the warmth of family and the sound of giggles fill the room—it's Christmas, after all!

The Great "Foil Santa" Mix-Up

It was the big holiday decoration contest in the neighborhood, and little Oliver wanted to help his dad win. This year, they were going all out! Oliver's dad had ordered a giant inflatable Santa to be the main attraction for their display.

When the big box arrived, Oliver was so excited he could hardly stand still. He looked up at his dad with a big grin and asked, "Dad, can I help with the inflation?"

Dad smiled, "Of course, buddy! We'll get Santa up in no time."

But Oliver didn't know what "inflation" meant. He thought it had something to do with making things fly, like balloons. So, while Dad was untangling the Christmas lights, Oliver ran to the kitchen and grabbed a roll of shiny foil. He started wrapping Santa in the foil, bit by bit.

Dad turned around and froze. There was Oliver, carefully covering Santa like a giant baked potato. "Ollie, what are you doing?" Dad asked, trying not to laugh.

Oliver looked up, very serious. "Dad, I'm trying to make Santa *inflatable*! Shiny stuff makes balloons float, right?"

Dad couldn't help it—he burst out laughing. "No, buddy, inflation means we have to blow him up with *air*, not foil!"

Oliver paused, looking between the foil and Santa, then shrugged. "Well, he still looks shiny. Maybe it'll help!"

They both laughed so hard that the neighbors peeked over the fence to see what was going on. In the end, they decided to leave some of the foil on Santa, just for fun. That night, their yard had the shiniest, funniest Santa on the block.

Oliver proudly told everyone who passed by, "This Santa's extra special, thanks to my shiny powers!"

The Mrs. Claus Discovery

It was Christmas Eve, and the Johnsons had invited their new neighbors, the Petersons, over for dinner. Everything was perfect— Christmas carols were playing, the fireplace was glowing, and everyone was having a good time. Then, little Emily decided it was time to ask Mrs. Peterson a very *important* question.

Emily marched right up to Mrs. Peterson, who was sitting near the tree, and asked, loud enough for everyone to hear, "Mrs. Peterson, are you Mrs. Claus?"

The room went silent for a moment, and then everyone turned to look at Mrs. Peterson. She blinked, a bit surprised, then smiled warmly. "Why do you think that, dear?" she asked.

"Because you have all the white hair, and you laugh like 'ho ho ho!' Just like Mrs. Claus!" Emily said, trying her best to sound like Santa.

Mrs. Peterson laughed, and Mr. Peterson leaned in with a twinkle in his eye. "Well, that's because she *is* Mrs. Claus, but it's a secret," he said.

Emily's eyes grew huge, and she gasped. "Wow!" She turned to her brother, "Jeremy, Mrs. Claus is *real*, and she's here for dinner!"

The whole room erupted in laughter, and Mrs. Peterson gave Emily a wink. From that night on, Mrs. Peterson became "Mrs. Claus" for all the neighborhood kids, and Emily was so proud to have discovered Santa's best-kept secret.

The Great Hamster Escape

It was "Show and Tell" day, and Timmy had brought his hamster, Max, to class. Timmy was excited to show everyone how cute Max was. Mr. Benson, the teacher, made one thing very clear—*Max had to stay in his cage*.

Timmy nodded and promised. But halfway through his presentation, he thought it would be more fun if everyone got to see Max up close. So, Timmy opened the cage door just a little bit to give Max a pat.

But Max had other ideas. As soon as the door opened, Max shot out of the cage like a rocket! The class went wild. Timmy lunged for Max, but Max dashed under desks and between bookbags.

Mr. Benson jumped up, pointing, and shouted, "Get him! Get him!" He even stood on his chair, looking out for Max.

Max raced past the art supplies, and someone's lunchbox flew into the air. Kids were diving left and right, trying to catch the speedy little hamster. At one point, Bella called out, "He's heading for the crayons!" and half the class was on their hands and knees, crawling after him.

Finally, Max zoomed across the room and, as if he decided enough was enough, ran right back to his cage. Timmy quickly shut the door, and everyone cheered.

Mr. Benson slowly stepped down from his chair, straightened his tie, and said, "And *that*, class, is why we keep hamster cages *closed*." The whole room burst into laughter, and Timmy gave Max a proud smile. Max may have had his great escape, but Timmy knew they'd be telling this story in the cafeteria for weeks.

Holiday Hijinks for Teens

Welcome to Holiday Hijinks, a section designed especially for the teens who love a good laugh! Whether you're hanging out with friends or just need a break from schoolwork, these jokes are the perfect way to add a dash of humor to your holiday season. This collection of puns, riddles, and one-liners is crafted with you in mind—fun, witty, and full of that teen edge.

Get ready to find jokes that speak your language. We've got plenty of sarcastic reindeer, elf pranks, and even some jokes that may just have you rolling your eyes—but in a good way. Whether you're chilling on your phone, texting your friends, or gathered with family over holiday dinner, these jokes are sure to spark some laughs and keep the festive vibe going strong.

So, sit back, grab some cocoa, and get ready to dive into the most epic collection of holiday humor for teens. Let's see if these jokes can make even the most "cool and collected" teen crack a smile.

The holidays just got a whole lot funnier!

Christmas Puns

Why did Santa get a parking ticket on Christmas Eve?
Because he left his sleigh in a "no fly zone!"

Why did Santa switch to headphones?
So he could keep it on the "down sleigh!"

Why did Santa upgrade his sleigh to a new model?
He needed more horsepower for all the new games!

Why did Santa get kicked out of the gym?
He kept dropping the "sleigh-bells!"

Why did Santa stop eating candy canes?
He was trying to avoid a "sticky situation!"

Why does Santa avoid online shopping?
He prefers "sleigh-mail!"

Why was Mrs. Claus worried about Santa?
He kept acting like he had "wrap star" ambitions!

Why did Santa bring a pencil to the party?
He wanted to "draw" a little attention!

Food Jokes

Why did the snowman break up with the snow-woman?
He felt like she was giving him the cold shoulder!

Why did the Christmas cookie break up with its frosting?
It needed a little more "space" to crumble!

What did the Christmas ornament say to the tree?
"I'm just here to hang out!"

Why did the reindeer refuse to play video games?
It didn't want to get "stag-nant!"

Why did Frosty start a band?
He wanted to add some "cool" beats to the holidays!

What did the elf say after a breakup?
"I'm 'elf-sufficient' anyway!"

Why did the mistletoe reject the snowman's proposal?
She said she needed to "branch" out a bit more!

Why was Cupid jealous of Santa?
Because Santa gets all the "claus!"

26

School and Teen Life Puns

Why did the teenager refuse to help decorate the Christmas tree?
It wasn't in their "spruce" of interests!

Why was the candy cane so good at school?
Because it always stayed "sharp!"

Why did the student elf ace the geography test?
Because he had a great "North Pole" reference!

Why do teenagers always get first pick of the Christmas cookies?
They have "sleigh-gendary" timing!

Why do teenagers love snowball fights?
It's the only kind of "throwing shade" allowed during winter!

Why did the reindeer skip school?
Because it already had a "sleigh day!"

Why did the Christmas tree join the math club?
It wanted to work on its "root" problems!

Social Media and Technology Puns

What do elves post on social media?
Their "elfies" from the North Pole!

Why was Rudolph so good at Snapchat?
Because he always knew how to "filter"
out the best moments!

Why did Frosty decide to become an influencer?
Because he wanted to boost his "ice-tagram" followers!

Why did Santa's helper start a YouTube channel?
He wanted to share his "elf-improvement" tips!

Why did the reindeer start a podcast?
To "sleigh" the competition with hilarious holiday stories!

Why did the snowflake open a Twitter account?
To share all its "flake-tastic" moments!

Why did Mrs. Claus go viral on TikTok?
She nailed the "cookie dance" challenge!

Why was Frosty so bad at texting?
He kept getting "cold" replies!

Miscellaneous Puns

**What do you call a holiday concert
performed by ghosts?**
A "boo-tiful" Christmas carol!

**Why was the Christmas wrapping paper
so talkative?**
Because it had a lot to "unwrap!"

Why did the snowflake join the basketball team?
Because it knew how to make some "frosty" shots!

Why didn't the sleigh make any noise?
Because it was on "silent night" mode!

Why do elves always make great comedians?
They have a real knack for "sleigh-ing" the audience!

How do snowflakes get around town?
They take the "ice-cycles!"

What kind of music do Christmas trees like?
They love listening to "rocking around the tree!"

Introduction to Riddles for Holiday Hijinks

Think you've got what it takes to solve some festive puzzles? It's time to challenge your friends and family with these creative and fun holiday-themed riddles. We've gathered a mix of brain-teasers that are perfect for anyone who loves putting their wits to the test. From Santa's secrets to reindeer mysteries, these riddles are sure to keep you thinking—and laughing—all holiday season long. Whether you're just chilling with friends or trying to keep everyone entertained during a long car ride, these riddles will be a hit. Ready to riddle? Let's go!

Teen Life and Relationships Riddles

What's the best gift a teen could give to their sibling for Christmas?
Their phone charger back!

What do you call it when two Christmas ornaments start dating?
A holiday "hook-up."

Why did the mistletoe break up with the pine tree?
It felt like their relationship was getting too "sappy."

What did one snowflake say to the other while falling?
"I'm falling for you!"

Why don't Christmas lights ever get lonely?
Because they always hang out together!

Why did the gingerbread man go on a date?
He needed someone to "spice" up his life.

Why did Santa write his crush a love letter?
He wanted her to be his "Claus" mate.

Gaming and Pop Culture Riddles

Why did Santa create a gaming profile?
So he could "sleigh" in every game he played!

Why don't elves play online games?
Because they keep losing "connection" at the North Pole!

Why is Santa always good at strategy games?
Because he's used to planning routes all year!

How do elves unlock new skills for toy-making?
They "level up" by earning extra candy points!

Why was Frosty the Snowman a bad gamer?
Because he always melted under pressure!

Why did Santa rage quit his game?
He couldn't handle being "elf-liminated"!

Why did the elf stop playing VR games?
He got tangled up in the "sleigh cords"!

Gaming and Pop Culture Riddles

Why is Frosty always good at puzzles?
Because he knows how to keep his "cool" under pressure!

What does Mrs. Claus say whenever she wins a game?
"I guess I'm the real 'Claus' for celebration!"

Why did the elf decide to start a podcast about gaming?
He wanted to share tips on how to
"wrap up" those tough levels !

Why did Santa invest in a gaming chair?
So he could be "well-seated" for his sleigh missions!

Why did the reindeer stream his gaming sessions?
To show everyone he's got "antler-nate" skills!

Why did Santa's elves challenge each other to a gaming tournament?
To see who could "wrap up" the competition!

Introduction to One-Liners for Teens

Ready for some fast laughs? These one-liners are short, snappy, and perfect for anyone who loves a good joke without the long setup. Whether you're looking to drop some humor into a group chat, lighten up a family gathering, or impress your friends with your quick wit, these one-liners are bound to deliver.

They're perfect for capturing the holiday spirit while adding a modern, teen twist—think gaming, relationships, and all the ups and downs of teen life. So, scroll down and get ready to laugh at the speed of a text notification.

Let's keep the holiday vibe going strong—one quick joke at a time!

Christmas and Holiday One-Liners

Santa delivered a chill Christmas—literally, it's freezing!

Santa switched to LED lights to save those "sleigh-bills"!

Snowman's favorite food? Anything on "ice."

Gingerbread men stay fit by running away from
being eaten—ultimate motivation!

The Christmas tree was a show-off
because it knew it was "lit."

Santa's always got time for a good "wrap" session.

The North Pole has one rule:
Stay "frosty" under pressure.

Santa used a smartphone to "sleigh"
his to-do list faster!

Candy canes are just peppermint sticks
having a twisted time!

What do snowmen do in the off-season?
Chill, obviously.

Christmas and Holiday One-Liners

Told my crush I was cold—they gave me their hoodie.
Best Christmas ever!

Holiday gift for friends?
A coupon for "one get-out-of-drama-free card"!

The elf got ghosted—too "elf-centered."

Holiday parties are great—until you run out of
hiding spots when your crush walks in.

They said dress festive, so I wore a hoodie—
the official gear of comfort.

Texting my crush during holidays is
my way to "wrap" up my nerves.

Friends bought matching pajamas to sleigh
the group photo game!

Teen relationships are like gingerbread houses
—sweet but one wrong move, and they crumble.

Passions and Hobbies One-Liners

Winter break hobby:
Building snowmen that dress better than me.

Santa took up knitting—
everyone's getting "sweater" this year.

Told my mom I wanted to bake—
she gave me chores.
Classic mix-up!

Ice skating is like life:
glide until you fall, then get back up.

This holiday, my hobby is avoiding any
chore that requires leaving bed.

My dog's hobby?
Finding the hidden Christmas cookies—
total "paws-on" activity!

Snow angels?
Just my kind of creative expression—falling with style.

Passions and Hobbies One-Liners

Why do Christmas trees always look so confident?
Because they know they're "lit" from top to bottom.

What do reindeer put on before taking a selfie?
A "moose-filter," obviously!

Why did the Christmas tree join the choir?
It wanted to "branch out" into caroling.

Why was Mrs. Claus annoyed at Santa's party?
He kept "snowing" off his dance moves.

Why did Santa get lost? He took the wrong "elf-turn!"
Why did the gingerbread man join the gym?
To get that "dough-sired" shape for the holidays.

Why did the office Christmas party get so awkward?
Because everyone got a little too into the
"sleigh-ing" of drinks!

What do you call a holiday where everyone just relaxes?
A "no-elf-given" kind of day.

Holiday Story Time for Teens

Gather 'round, everyone! Whether you're sitting by the fireplace, lounging with friends, or just looking for a good laugh, these holiday-themed stories are made for sharing. Perfect for a Christmas evening get-together or a festive hangout, each of these tales captures the fun, awkward, and hilarious moments that make the holiday season so memorable.

So, grab some hot cocoa, sit back, and get ready for some laughs—these stories are sure to bring out smiles and giggles, even from the most "too cool for Christmas" teen in the room!

The Secret Santa Prank Gone Wrong

It all started when Jason decided to be the funniest guy in the entire school by pulling the ultimate prank during the annual Secret Santa exchange. His best friend, Emma, was his Secret Santa recipient, and he thought it would be hilarious to give her the worst possible gift: a box that looked enormous on the outside but was filled with nothing but crumpled newspaper, topped off with a single used sock. The plan was perfect—or at least, Jason thought it was.

When the day arrived, Jason proudly handed Emma her massive gift box in front of the whole class. Everyone gathered around as Emma, with a playful grin, began unwrapping layer after layer of crumpled newspaper, making dramatic faces as if she were expecting something amazing. The class giggled, and Jason felt his confidence grow. "Just wait till she gets to the sock!" he thought, trying not to laugh out loud.

But then came the twist—Emma finally reached the sock at the bottom of the box. Instead of being mad or even mildly annoyed, she raised the sock above her head and shouted, "This is exactly what I needed!

My little brother's been stealing mine for weeks!" Without missing a beat, she put the sock on her hand like a puppet and began doing an entire comedy routine with it. The whole class erupted in laughter, and suddenly Jason's prank had backfired—Emma stole the show with a used sock! Jason couldn't believe it; his prank had made her more popular than ever.

Now, whenever Jason tries to prank Emma, she just raises her sock puppet and says, "Oh, I hope it's a match for Mr. Sockington here!"

He knows better than to underestimate her again—she can turn any prank into a comedy act of her own.

The Holiday Hoodie Mix-Up

It was the last day of school before winter break, and everybody knew what that meant: the holiday hoodie tradition. Every year, the students would come to school dressed in their most over-the-top festive hoodies—the uglier, the better. Light-up reindeer noses, miniature stockings stitched to the sleeves, and even jingle bells hanging from the drawstrings—it was all about who could be the most extra.

Mia had been planning for weeks. She had the most hideous holiday hoodie ready, complete with flashing lights and a sound chip that played "Jingle Bells" whenever she moved her arms. She was ready to win the unofficial "ugliest hoodie" contest for the third year in a row. The only problem was, Mia wasn't exactly a morning person, and in her groggy haze that morning, she grabbed her brother's plain, boring gray hoodie by mistake.

It wasn't until she was halfway to school that she realized her mistake. "Oh no," Mia thought, "I'm doomed!" She looked around the bus, noticing everyone else in their festive gear—Santa hats, antler headbands, and sweaters covered in sparkles. She tugged her plain gray hoodie closer, feeling like a holiday failure.

But when she got to school, something unexpected happened. Her friends saw her plain hoodie and immediately decided she was making some kind of cool, ironic statement. "Whoa, Mia, that's genius! The anti-ugly holiday hoodie!" one of them said, while another added, "So minimalist, so bold!" Before she knew it, people were complimenting her for "standing out by not standing out." By the end of the day, half the school was talking about how "chill" Mia looked in her understated holiday gear.

Mia didn't win the ugly hoodie contest that year—but she did win the award for "Most Unexpected Trendsetter." And her brother still hasn't gotten his hoodie back.

The Gingerbread House Disaster

Tyler wasn't exactly known for his culinary skills, but when his crush, Abby, invited him to her family's annual gingerbread house-making party, he couldn't say no. He figured, "How hard could it be? It's just cookies and icing, right?" He arrived at Abby's house, determined to impress her with his gingerbread architecture. The only problem? Tyler had never made a gingerbread house in his life.

He started confidently enough, slapping pieces of gingerbread together with globs of icing. But as the minutes passed, things took a turn. His icing was too runny, his walls kept sliding apart, and somehow, he ended up with half a roof that looked like it had been hit by a blizzard. Meanwhile, Abby's gingerbread house looked like something straight out of a Christmas card—perfectly decorated with tiny candies and even a little icing snowman out front.

Trying to salvage his collapsing mess, Tyler added more icing—lots more icing. It worked for a second, but then the whole house gave way and collapsed in a sticky heap. Tyler sighed, realizing his attempt to impress Abby had turned into a disaster. He looked over at Abby, ready to apologize for the mess, but to his surprise, she was laughing—hard.

"Tyler, that's the most epic gingerbread disaster I've ever seen!" she said, grabbing a piece of broken gingerbread and offering it to him. "Here, let's just eat it—at least it tastes good, right?" Tyler took the piece and smiled. Maybe his house had crumbled, but at least he got to make Abby laugh—and that was better than any perfect gingerbread creation.

From that day on, Tyler became known as the "Gingerbread Demolition Expert."

And the next year, Abby invited him back—this time to make gingerbread "ruins," which, to be fair, Tyler was really good at.

Festive Vibes for Young Adults

Welcome to Festive Vibes, the section that brings a blend of witty humor and a little sarcasm—perfect for young adults who appreciate a clever laugh. Whether you're celebrating the holidays with friends, stuck at work trying to stay in the festive spirit, or just relaxing with a cup of coffee, these jokes are crafted for you. We've got holiday-themed humor with a grown-up twist, touching on relationships, social media, office life, and everything in between.

This section will help you break the ice at holiday parties, spark some laughs in your group chat, and maybe even lighten the mood when family gatherings get a little too real. From clever puns to playful sarcasm, get ready for a collection of jokes that will make even the most sophisticated grin crack.

So, kick back, get comfortable, and let's add some holiday cheer—with a dash of young adult flair!

Relationship Puns

Why did the snowman break up with the snow-woman?
He found her a little too "flaky."

What did the mistletoe say to the Christmas lights?
"Let's hang out and make things shine."

Why did the reindeer couple break up during Christmas?
They couldn't "sleigh" their differences.

What do Christmas lights say when they get engaged?
"We're just here to shine together!"

**Why did the gingerbread cookie propose
at the holiday party?**
Because it found someone who was its "perfect bake!"

Why did Frosty call off his date with the snow-woman?
He got "cold feet."

Why did the Christmas bell start dating the wreath?
It was ready to "ring in" the holidays
with someone special.

University Life Puns

**Why did the student put up Christmas lights
in their dorm room?**
To help "brighten" up their GPA.

**Why did the professor give out extra credit
during the holidays?**
To spread a little "academic cheer."

**Why did the student stay up all night
making a gingerbread model?**
It was their "final bake-signment!"

Why was the library so quiet during the holidays?
Even the books were "shelved" with care.

Why did the snowman audit a chemistry class?
He wanted to learn more about "solid" relationships.

Early Job Experience Puns

Why did the elf intern get a raise?
He was really good at "wrapping up" his projects.

Why did the gingerbread man quit his first job?
He couldn't handle the "crummy" hours.

Why was the office so cold at the holiday temp job?
Because they had a "frosty" boss.

Why did the new intern love wrapping gifts?
It was "present-tially" the easiest job.

Why did Santa hire a snowflake for the job?
Because it was a "flake-tastic" fit for seasonal help.

Why did the young adult stay late at the holiday job?
To earn a "jingle" bonus.

What did the Christmas lights say at the staff meeting?
"Let's not leave anyone in the dark!"

Social Media and Pop Culture Puns

Why did Santa start a TikTok account?
To share his "sleigh-ing" dance moves.

Why was Rudolph trending on Twitter?
He spilled the tea about the North Pole—
it was "glow-rific!"

Why did the Christmas cookie post a selfie?
Because it wanted to show it was "baked to perfection."

What did Frosty caption his Instagram photo?
"Ice to meet you!"

Why did Santa's workshop go viral?
It had all the "elves-thetics!"

Why did Mrs. Claus trend on TikTok?
She posted a "baking reel" that got everyone "frosty."

Miscellaneous Puns

Why did the ornament get promoted?
Because it "hung in there" through the tough times.

Why did the gingerbread man refuse a
second helping of icing?
He was watching his "sugar-coat."

Why did Santa's helper start meditating?
To stay "jolly" even when the work piled up.

Why did the holiday candles throw a party?
To have a "lit" time.

Why did the bell choir get so
many gigs during December?
They knew how to "ring in" the season perfectly.

Introduction to Riddles for Young Adults

Get ready to sharpen your mind and test your wit with our collection of riddles designed just for young adults! Whether you're looking to outsmart your friends, add some flair to a holiday gathering, or simply enjoy a mental challenge while sipping on your favorite hot drink, these riddles will keep you entertained.

They bring a playful twist to everyday life—touching on relationships, university struggles, early job experiences, and, of course, the festive chaos of the holidays. These riddles are here to make you think, laugh, and maybe even roll your eyes, but in the best way possible. So, dive in, share them with friends, and see who can solve them first. The holiday fun is about to get a whole lot smarter!

Young Adult Riddles

I'm often empty, but I fill up every night at the bar.
What am I?
A wallet!

I'm late at night, always involve a group, and
rarely lead to a productive next morning.
What am I?
A Netflix binge!

What do you always look forward to, but once it starts,
you want it to end quickly?
A work meeting!

I'm the reason you stay awake in the morning and
stay up at night. What am I?
Coffee!

I'm great for meeting new people, but you usually end up
swiping away. What am I?
A dating app!

make you feel grown-up but often end in frustration, and
you're never sure if it's really worth it. What am I?
Filing taxes!

Young Adult Riddles

I'm something you take everywhere, never want to lose, and freak out if I go below 10%.
What am I?
A phone!

I'm something you pay for every month but pretend you know nothing about when it's time to split the bill.
What am I?
Streaming subscriptions!

I'm great for taking your stress away until I arrive. Then I just pile it back on. What am I?
A delivery order you can't afford!

I'm something you love to take selfies with, but hate when I remind you of reality. What am I?
A mirror!

What always makes you feel ambitious at night, but regrets in the morning?
Setting early alarms!

Relationship Riddles

What do you break before you can use it,
especially during the holidays?
A wishbone!

What has a ring but no fingers, and often
marks a holiday promise?
A bell!

You share me during the holidays, and I only grow
the more you give. What am I?
Love!

You'll find me under a special doorway during Christmas,
encouraging romance. What am I?
Mistletoe!

I come in many colors, I am tall or small, and I
light up when you show me love.
What am I?
A candle!

I'm known to "tie the knot," but you'll need me
to hang a wreath. What am I?
A ribbon!

Relationship Riddles

I'm cold but bring people together. You can throw me, but I never break. What am I?

A snowball!

I am something that has no form but connects people, especially during holiday gatherings. What am I?

A hug!

I make you laugh, give warmth, and can often lead to friendship or love. What am I?

A smile!

What holiday symbol can lead to a kiss but never says a word?

Mistletoe!

I am something that often lights up at the perfect moment, especially during the holidays, to make memories last forever. What am I?

A camera!

University Life Riddles

What does everyone have but often loses
during finals week?
Sleep!

I am something that you don't want to see on
your university transcript. What am I?
An "F"!

What can you find at the library that
doesn't require a library card?
Knowledge!

I can be borrowed but never returned,
especially during class time. What am I?
A pen!

I am something you have to write but hope to get
hrough quickly, and I usually appear during the holidays.
What am I?
An exam!

What keeps a student warm during winter
but isn't made of wool?
A heated argument about grades!

University Life Riddles

I'm something you need to pass, but you never
want to take me. What am I?
A test!

I'm always part of a group project but never contribute.
Who am I?
That one group member!

I am something you get after four years but
never actually see. What am I?
Student debt payoff!

I'm invisible, but I cause stress,
especially at 11:59 PM. What am I?
A deadline!

What takes four years to earn and a lifetime to pay off?
A student loan!

One-Liners for Young Adults

Looking for some quick laughs to brighten up your holiday season? These one-liners are designed to be short, snappy, and straight to the point—perfect for sharing with friends, dropping into a group chat, or keeping the conversation light at holiday gatherings. From the ups and downs of early job experiences to the quirky moments of relationships and the chaos of university life, these one-liners touch on everything that young adults can relate to.

Whether you're at a holiday party or just trying to lighten the mood during a long workday, these jokes will deliver laughs in just a few words. So, get ready for a dose of humor that's easy to remember and impossible not to share!

Holiday One-Liners

Christmas lights: because nothing says festive
like an electrical hazard.

I put up a tree—now my cat thinks it's a new jungle gym.

Eggnog: my one true seasonal weakness.

Untangling Christmas lights counts
as holiday cardio, right?

I told Santa I wanted a break from adulthood;
he just laughed.

My holiday spirit is directly proportional
to the number of cookies I've had.

My idea of "holiday cheer"
is getting to wear pajamas all day.

Why do holiday decorations always take longer
to put away than they do to put up?

If I wrap a present well, I feel like I've accomplished
enough for the day.

Relationship One-Liners

Nothing says 'I love you' like
sharing your Netflix password.

My crush got me socks—guess that's a
'cold feet' kind of gift.

Christmas is for love; Valentine's is for regrets.

The only thing I'm cuddling this winter is
my electric blanket.

Holiday romances are great until you realize
they expire with the year.

Is it still called 'ghosting' if it happens
during a holiday party?

Mistletoe is just a polite way of forcing a
romantic encounter in December.

The real test of a relationship?
Surviving holiday family gatherings together.

University Life One-Liners

My GPA and my Christmas cheer are both running low.

I'm in debt, but at least my dorm has fairy lights.

Finals week: spreading cheer one
panic attack at a time.

If Santa could pay my tuition,
I'd really believe in miracles.

Who needs New Year's resolutions when
student loans are forever?

Winter break: the only time I miss school is for
the free heating.

Studying for finals is like wrapping gifts:
messy, stressful, and full of surprises.

I'm dreaming of a degree-less Christmas...
because I failed all my finals.

Holiday sales?
More like 'let's distract broke college students' sales.

University Life One-Liners

My holiday bonus was just a reminder to be grateful I have a job.

The best part of my temp job is knowing it ends soon.

Holiday shifts mean getting paid to pretend I'm happy.

I didn't realize "team bonding" meant exchanging tacky mugs.

Holiday customer service: a test in patience and fake smiles.

My boss gave me a fruitcake for the holidays— I guess they know how I feel about work.

Nothing says 'entry-level job' like getting the honor of cleaning up after the office party.

Social and Miscellaneous One-Liners

The holidays: when I pretend my baking
skills are Instagram-worthy.

Holiday parties are just adult group projects with snacks.

I eat gingerbread houses because building isn't my thing.

I'm only singing carols for the hot cocoa and cookies.

Christmas shopping: my yearly exercise
in panic and poor decisions.

If you don't embarrass yourself at least once
at a holiday party, did you even attend?

Trying to stay on a diet during the holidays is like
bringing a spoon to a knife fight.

My idea of a holiday miracle is finding parking
at the mall in December.

New Year's resolution:
survive holiday gatherings without starting an argument.

Holiday Laughter Ahead!

Whether you're sitting around the fireplace with friends or chilling after a holiday dinner, these funny stories are made for sharing. Packed with humor that young adults will recognize from their own lives, these tales are perfect for reading aloud to bring on some laughs and relatable "oh no" moments.

Grab your favorite hot drink, settle in, and get ready to share a few stories that capture the chaos, awkwardness, and hilarity of being young during the holiday season!

The Gift Exchange That Went Way Too Far

Sophia and her group of friends had been doing a "White Elephant" gift exchange every year since high school. You know, the kind where everyone brings something silly, and then people get to steal gifts from each other? It had always been a lot of fun, but this year, something had changed—everyone seemed to have upped the ante on ridiculousness.

It started off simple enough: a pair of socks with Santa doing yoga, a mug shaped like a llama, and a plant that someone had clearly forgotten to water. Then came the box that Sophia had been eyeing all night. It was huge, shiny, and covered in way more wrapping paper than was necessary.

When it was her turn, she quickly grabbed the box. Everyone watched as she tore off the paper. Inside, she found... a blender. Not just any blender—it was a top-of-the-line, super fancy blender that had clearly cost way more than the usual $20 limit.

Everyone oohed and aahed, and Sophia couldn't believe her luck—until her friend, Kevin, smirked and said, "Wait, open the card." Inside was a handwritten note: "Congrats on your new smoothie obsession! P.S. It's actually just a box—enjoy the socks inside."

Sophia reached into the blender box and pulled out a pair of the fuzziest, tackiest Christmas socks she'd ever seen. The room erupted in laughter. As it turned out, the real blender belonged to Kevin's mom, and he'd just borrowed the box. The socks were the real gift—he'd found them at the dollar store five minutes before the exchange. Sophia's still plotting how to outdo him next year.

The Cooking Catastrophe

Liam wanted to impress his roommates by making a full holiday dinner. They'd all agreed to stay on campus instead of going home for winter break, which meant they'd have to find their own way to bring some holiday cheer into their shared apartment. Liam, being overly confident in his non-existent cooking skills, thought, "How hard could it be?"

He had watched about ten minutes of a cooking video and was sure he had it down. But things started going wrong almost immediately. First, he didn't have half the spices the recipe called for, so he substituted with the only things available—hot sauce and ketchup. The turkey didn't fit in the oven, so he wedged it in, thinking it would shrink when it cooked (spoiler alert: it didn't). And somehow, while attempting to mash the potatoes, Liam managed to splatter half of them across the ceiling.

Finally, after what felt like a hundred hours of chaos, dinner was ready—or at least, what could pass for dinner. The turkey looked a little... burnt. Okay, more than a little. The potatoes were more like glue, and the gravy was unidentifiable.

But Liam's roommates, being good sports, sat down at the table anyway. They all took a bite at the same time, and the silence that followed was legendary. Then his roommate Rachel, always the honest one, said, "Liam, I think I just tasted charcoal... and regret."

They all ended up laughing hysterically, abandoning the disaster of a meal and ordering pizza instead. From then on, Liam was strictly assigned to "dish duty" whenever holiday dinners were involved.

The Holiday Roommate Surprise

Megan had a brilliant idea for her roommates: a surprise holiday decoration overhaul for their apartment. She had seen enough Pinterest boards to know exactly how to transform their dreary college living space into a winter wonderland. She imagined twinkling lights, a perfectly decorated mini tree, and maybe even a hot chocolate bar— something that would make everyone feel like they were in a Hallmark movie.

The execution, however, was a little more chaotic than her Pinterest dreams. Megan recruited her roommate, Alex, for help, but Alex was more interested in taste-testing the marshmallows than actually decorating. They started with the lights.

Simple enough, right? Well, not exactly. The lights turned into a massive, tangled nightmare that Megan swore was possessed—it took them an hour just to untangle, and then when they finally plugged them in, half the bulbs were dead.

Determined not to let that ruin the vibe, Megan moved on to the tree. They had found a tiny, slightly sad artificial tree on clearance at the dollar store. They decorated it with whatever they could find: some popcorn on thread, a few mismatched ornaments, and a homemade star they fashioned out of aluminum foil and coat hangers.

The tree leaned dangerously to one side, but they decided it had "character."

The final touch was the pièce de résistance—a fake snow spray that Megan thought would really make the place pop. She went to town with the can, spraying it on the windows, the tree, the table... and accidentally, Alex's cat, Mittens, who had wandered into the line of fire.

Mittens was not impressed and quickly disappeared under the couch, leaving behind a trail of tiny, snowy paw prints.

When their other roommates returned, they were greeted by a leaning tree, tangled lights half-lit, a marshmallow-covered Alex, and a disgruntled cat who now looked like he was part snowman. There was a moment of silence before everyone burst out laughing.

"Wow, you really nailed the 'post-apocalyptic winter wonderland' look," one of the roommates quipped, snapping a photo of the chaos.

It wasn't perfect, but it was their holiday mess, and that made it just right. The snow-sprayed paw prints on the carpet, they all agreed, were just part of the apartment's festive charm.

From that year forward, "DIY Holiday Cat-Snow Disaster" became an annual tradition, and even Mittens had grown to tolerate his role as the unofficial snow-kitty mascot.

Holiday Cheers for the Grown-Ups

Welcome to the "Holiday Cheers for the Grown-Ups" section—where the jokes get a little sharper, the humor gets a little more real, and the festive spirit comes with a side of sarcasm. This collection is made for those who've seen a few holiday seasons come and go, and know that behind every "Silent Night" is a pile of last-minute wrapping, awkward family gatherings, and endless to-do lists.

Whether you're looking to lighten the mood at an office party, add some humor to a friends-only holiday gathering, or simply find a reason to laugh amid the seasonal madness, these jokes are here to deliver.

From the ups and downs of family life to the stress of holiday shopping and the humor in juggling work parties with holiday prep, this section has it all. So, pour yourself a glass of your favorite holiday beverage, kick back, and let's find some laughs in the chaos.

After all, being an adult during the holidays is anything but easy—so we might as well laugh about it!

Holiday Puns

Why did Santa get into real estate?

He wanted to branch out into the "ho-ho-home" market.

Why did I wrap my holiday stress in tinsel?

So at least it sparkles!

What's a Christmas tree's least favorite month?

Sep-timber—because that's when people start chopping them down.

Why does Rudolph always take his job seriously?

He's got too much at "stake"—or rather, at "sleigh!"

Why did Mrs. Claus take up knitting?

To keep Santa "in stitches" all year long.

Why did Frosty get a sun lamp for Christmas?

To work on his "chill" tan.

Why are snowmen so great at parties?

Because they're always "cool" under pressure.

What did Santa say when he ran out of wrapping paper?

"Looks like I'm about to 'wrap' up my creativity!"

Family Life Puns

Why do family gatherings feel like playing Jenga?

One wrong word and the whole thing topples.

What did the family say when they finished putting up the decorations?

"Let's see how long it takes before the cat wrecks it all!"

Why did the parents cover the gifts in aluminum foil?

To make sure they were "foiled" against peeking eyes.

Why did Grandma bring a whistle to the holiday dinner?

To call a "time-out" during the political debates.

What do parents and Christmas lights have in common?

Both work really hard but never get untangled.

Why did Uncle Joe bring a fruitcake to the family dinner?

Because it's the one thing everyone "passes" on.

Why did my mom bring three different desserts?

To avoid another "sugar-coated" argument from last year.

Why do family board games always end in chaos?

Because it's never just "games"—it's family history.

Work and Office Party Puns

Why did the office holiday party need a referee?
Too many people were crossing "wine" boundaries.

What's the difference between the office coffee and the holiday party punch?
One keeps you awake, and the other makes you wish you weren't.

What's an office worker's favorite Christmas carol?
"I'm Dreaming of a Paid Holiday."

Why did the corporate Christmas tree look so stressed out
Because it heard it was getting "trimmed" again this year!

Why did I bring cookies to the office party?
To "sweeten" up my request for more vacation days.

What's the most overused phrase at the office holiday party?
"I'm only here for the food."

Why did I volunteer to plan the office holiday games?
Because it counts as a "team-building" on my resume.

Holiday Shopping Puns

Why does Christmas shopping feel like cardio?
Because nothing burns calories like the
panic of finding the last toy on the shelf.

Why was the gift-wrapping aisle so crowded?
Everyone was trying to "wrap" their minds
around what to buy.

**Why did the credit card break up with me
after the holidays?**
It couldn't handle the "emotional charge."

What's a shopper's favorite holiday workout?
Cardio followed by card-declining.

Why did my holiday budget end up on the naughty list?
Because it was completely "blown" away by gift-giving.

Why did my wallet take a vacation in January?
It needed to recover from the holiday "overcharge."

Why did I hide my receipts in the cookie jar?
So no one would find out the true cost of holiday cheer.

Social Life and Relationships Puns

What did the mistletoe say to the singles?
"I'm just hanging out—don't mind me!"

Why did I bring my partner to the holiday family reunion?
To deflect all the questions about life choices.

Why did the snowman refuse to go on a date?
He was tired of all the "cold shoulders."

What's worse than getting socks for Christmas?
Giving socks and realizing your partner
was expecting jewelry.

Why did I try to flirt at the holiday party?
Because mistletoe makes me think I have superpowers.

Why did my partner bring me to a New Year's Eve party?
To make sure someone was there to hold their
drink while they took selfies.

Why is dating during the holidays like playing charades?
Because everyone's pretending to be more festive
than they really are.

Introduction to Riddles for Adults

The holiday season brings plenty of festive cheer—but it also brings its fair share of chaos, stress, and more than a few awkward moments.

What better way to navigate all of this than with some clever riddles that bring out your sharp wit?

These riddles are crafted for adults who enjoy a mental challenge while sharing a laugh, perfect for sparking conversation at a holiday party, breaking the ice at an office gathering, or just keeping your mind engaged during those long family dinners. With topics ranging from holiday madness to work, relationships, and life in general, these riddles will make you think twice, smile, and maybe even groan a little.

So grab your favorite holiday beverage, settle in, and get ready to challenge your friends and family with some seriously fun brainteasers!

Family and Social Riddles

What's always ready to erupt during a holiday
dinner but never needs a match?
An argument!

I am something that brings a mix of joy and dread
when we gather each holiday. What am I?
Family!

I'm always served at holiday dinners but
rarely welcomed. What am I?
Unsolicited advice!

What do you bring to a holiday dinner
but hope never comes up?
Politics!

I'm always full but never heavy, and the more people
share me, the more I grow. What am I?
Laughter!

What's always served warm, often spiced, and makes the
family gathering a little more tolerable?
Mulled wine!

Family and Social Riddles

Why did the employee bring a gift to the boss's office?
To get on the "nice" list!

I'm something you dread at work but pretend to love during December. What am I?
The office holiday party!

I am something you make every year, yet you break me by February. What am I?
A New Year's resolution!

I come at the end of the year, full of numbers and facts, making everyone realize where the money went. What am I?
An end-of-year financial report!

What do you call a work meeting held during December?
A "why-can't-we-all-be-on-vacation" gathering.

Why did the corporate tree have no decorations?
Budget cuts made it a "bare minimum" kind of year.

What's full of secrets, endless complaints, and is whispered between desks?
Office gossip!

Miscellaneous Riddles

I can be warm, I can be bitter, but I'm always shared between two people in winter. What am I?

A cup of hot cocoa!

I start with excitement and end with a kiss, but after that, it's back to real life. What am I?

New Year's Eve!

I am something that is easy to give, but hard to keep; and during the holidays, I often get broken. What am I?

A promise!

I can make you laugh, I can make you cry, but most importantly, I'm always available for small talk during holiday gatherings. What am I?

A glass of wine!

I am something you receive every month, even during the holidays, and no one looks forward to seeing me. What am I?

A bill!

One-Liners for Young Adults

Looking for some quick laughs to brighten up your holiday season? These one-liners are designed to be short, snappy, and straight to the point—perfect for sharing with friends, dropping into a group chat, or keeping the conversation light at holiday gatherings. From the ups and downs of early job experiences to the quirky moments of relationships and the chaos of university life, these one-liners touch on everything that young adults can relate to.

Whether you're at a holiday party or just trying to lighten the mood during a long workday, these jokes will deliver laughs in just a few words. So, get ready for a dose of humor that's easy to remember and impossible not to share!

Holiday-Themed One-Liners

My holiday spirit is directly tied to how much
mulled wine I've had.

The only thing I'm wrapping this year is myself in a
blanket until it's all over.

I put up holiday lights just to prove to
my neighbors that I'm trying.

Eggnog is proof that adults need
dessert drinks to survive December.

Christmas is magical, until it's time to
clean up all the wrapping paper.

Santa checks his list twice, but I still forgot to buy milk.

Untangling Christmas lights counts as cardio for the entire year

Family gatherings are just group projects with
more passive-aggressive comments.

Holiday dinners are 20% food and 80%
dodging awkward questions.

Nothing brings out family drama quite like a board
game after dinner.

Work and Office One-Liners

My holiday bonus was just a reminder that I
should probably get a new job.

"Dress festive" for the office party?
Hope they like my reindeer onesie.

Nothing says 'Happy Holidays' like the boss asking
if you can work Christmas Eve.

Holiday overtime is basically just adulting
with a festive twist.

I prefer my holiday bonuses in cash, but I'll settle
for candy canes too.

They said 'Christmas cheer'; I heard 'mandatory overtime'.

My partner and I agreed not to exchange gifts—so naturally, I
panicked and bought something.

Holiday shopping: because nothing says 'I love you'
like stress-spending.

The holidays are magical, but my
bank account seems to be disappearing faster.

Laughter with a Grown-Up Twist

The holiday season is full of moments that don't always go according to plan, and these stories capture that familiar chaos in all its glory.

Whether it's about navigating the festive whirlwind at work, dealing with family expectations, or just surviving the mishaps that come with holiday preparations, each story is sure to hit home with anyone who's been there and done that.

Settle in with a warm drink and get ready to laugh at the misadventures that remind us why we love—and sometimes dread—this time of year.

The Office Party Catastrophe

Mark had always dreaded the annual office Christmas party. It wasn't the mingling or the forced small talk that bothered him—it was the inevitable moment when his boss, Mr. Higgins, got a little too into the eggnog and insisted that everyone partake in "festive games." Last year, Mr. Higgins had convinced half the staff to do a conga line that snaked through the HR department, nearly toppling the Christmas tree.

This year, Mark was ready to fly under the radar, sipping his non-alcoholic punch in the corner. But his plan came to a screeching halt when Mr. Higgins spotted him.

"Mark! You've got the perfect build for this!" Higgins bellowed, dragging Mark towards the front. Apparently, this year's entertainment was a game called "Santa's Sleigh Pull." Mark, along with several other unfortunate coworkers, was outfitted with reindeer antlers and a red nose and asked to "pull" a makeshift sleigh—a red office chair—occupied by Mr. Higgins, who had donned a Santa hat.

Mark tried to be a good sport, but as he and his fellow "reindeer" began to pull Higgins across the floor, someone lost their footing. The entire group went down like dominoes, sending Mr. Higgins flying off the chair and straight into the refreshments table. Eggnog splashed everywhere, and the crowd collectively gasped before bursting into laughter. Higgins, surprisingly unharmed and covered in eggnog, simply raised his glass and shouted, "Now that's the holiday spirit!"

Mark couldn't help but laugh. It was chaos, but it was also the perfect way to wrap up another year of surviving the nine-to-five grind. After all, what's an office party without a little accidental slapstick?

The Holiday Light Show-Off

Lisa had always loved decorating for Christmas, but this year her neighbor Carl had turned it into a full-on competition. Carl had lights everywhere—his roof, his trees, even his mailbox had a mini light display that spelled out "Merry Christmas!" in flashing colors. It was like Carl had hired an electrician and a Broadway director to design his front yard. Lisa, naturally, couldn't let herself be outdone.

So, she set out to create a display that would put Carl's to shame. She bought strings of lights, inflatable reindeer, and even a giant blow-up Santa that waved from her front lawn. But when she tried to plug it all in, her entire house went dark. She'd blown a fuse. Not one to be deterred, Lisa called in reinforcements—her best friend Matt, who claimed he "knew a thing or two about wiring."

With Matt's help, they managed to get everything working again. The house was lit up like a carnival, and Lisa couldn't have been prouder—until she realized the lights were flickering in sync with the neighbor's Christmas playlist. Somehow, Matt had crossed wires, and Lisa's lights were now dancing to Carl's music.

Carl, standing on his lawn with a grin, shouted over, "Hey Lisa! Looks like we're in sync this year!" Lisa groaned, but she couldn't help laughing at the absurdity. In the end, the two neighbors decided to make it a team effort, and every night, they coordinated their displays. The entire block loved the show, and Lisa had to admit—it was more fun with a partner-in-crime.

The Holiday Dinner Disaster

Jack had promised his wife, Emma, that he would handle Christmas dinner this year. It was supposed to be a relaxing holiday—no stress, no worries, just Jack taking care of everything. How hard could it be? After all, it was just cooking, right?

The trouble began when Jack decided to "upgrade" their usual turkey with a fancy herb-crusted recipe he'd seen on TV. The problem? Jack didn't actually know what half the ingredients were, so he substituted freely. Parsley became dried basil, and when he couldn't find garlic cloves, he just dumped in garlic powder—lots of it. It smelled... interesting.

Things only got worse when it was time to make the gravy. Jack had seen chefs on TV using wine in their sauces, so he grabbed a bottle of red, not realizing that maybe a whole bottle was a bit excessive. The result was a thick, purplish gravy that smelled like a winery had crashed the dinner party. When Emma's parents arrived, they were greeted by a table full of "creative" dishes. The turkey was dry, the gravy was borderline inedible, and the mashed potatoes—well, Jack had somehow forgotten to peel them, so they were more like lumpy, sad chunks.

Emma tried to be supportive. "Well, at least you tried," she said, attempting to chew the leathery turkey. Her dad, always the jokester, took a bite of the gravy-covered potatoes and coughed, "I think I'm getting notes of... regret."

Jack sighed, but then they all burst into laughter. It wasn't the perfect dinner he'd imagined, but it was memorable. In the end, they ordered Chinese takeout, and everyone agreed it was the best decision of the night. Jack learned that the true spirit of Christmas dinner wasn't about impressing anyone—it was about sharing a meal, even if that meal came in takeout containers.

Golden Holiday Giggles

Welcome to the "Golden Holiday Giggles" section, specially crafted for those who have seen a lifetime of holiday seasons—both the merry and the messy.

This collection of jokes and humor is meant to spark memories, celebrate the timeless joys of the season, and add a little laughter to your gatherings. From reminiscing about simpler holiday traditions to joking about the grandkids' antics, these jokes are designed to be warm, witty, and relatable.

Whether you're enjoying a quiet evening by the fireplace, sharing a laugh at a holiday gathering, or just looking to add a bit more joy to the festive season, this section is here for you.

With humor that ranges from nostalgic reflections to the lighthearted challenges of growing older, we hope these jokes bring smiles and maybe even a few hearty chuckles. After all, the holidays are a time for laughter—and that's something we never outgrow!

I love old holiday movies—they remind me that even decades ago, people were just as stressed as we are!

Why do I tell the grandkids about my old holiday traditions? Because I want them to "wrap" their minds around how simple things used to be.

Golden Holiday Giggles

Why did Santa stop working out?
He realized round is a shape too!

Why do snowmen never get tired of winter?
Because they're "chill" all year round!

I told the Christmas lights to stay untangled this year
they just laughed and said, "In your dreams!"

Why was the Christmas tree so bad at knitting?
It kept dropping its "needles."

I asked my grandkids to help decorate for Christmas
they said, "Sure!" and decorated me with garland.

What do you call a retired reindeer?
"Un-deer-employed."

Why was Rudolph always invited to holiday parties?
He knew how to really "light" up a room!

**I put up the mistletoe, but it turns out my partner
only wants "toe"**
tally comfortable slippers.

Family and Tradition Puns

Grandkids are great at decorating
they put the star on top, and I supervise from the recliner.

Why do grandparents always get the best seats during holiday dinner?
We earned the right to "sit back and relax."

What's Grandma's favorite part of the holiday cookies?
The memories baked in... and the icing on top!

I made a holiday pie, but the grandkids thought it was "crusty enough to use as a Frisbee.

Family gatherings are like a good holiday sweater:
warm, cozy, and a little itchy at times.

Why did the turkey get invited back to every family meal?
Because it was always stuffed with love!

They say age is just a number, but I prefer the number
that comes with a senior discount.

I told my doctor I was staying active
he didn't know I meant chasing grandkids
around the Christmas tree.

Family and Tradition Puns

Why do seniors always get along with Santa?
We both love a good "nap" and a cookie or two!

I don't need an advent calendar
my knees click enough to count down to Christmas.

I've got all my holiday shopping done early this year!
Now if only I could remember where I put the gifts.

What did the rocking chair say to me on Christmas Eve?
"We're in this together—let's rock the night away!

My memory isn't what it used to be, but
I still remember how to bake the best holiday pie.
That's what matters!

The best part of getting older?
No one questions you when you go for seconds... or thirds.

I told my grandkids I used to walk miles in the snow to school
they just laughed and showed me their new snow boots.

Family and Tradition Puns

Why did I keep all my old holiday cards?
Because nothing says "tradition" like a drawer full of memories

I remember when we had to decorate the tree with popcorn.
The best part? Eating it afterward!

Why did the old record player come out for Christmas?
To give the holiday party a real "spin"!

I still think the best holiday gifts are homemade ones
especially if someone else makes them!

Remember when toys didn't need batteries?
Now that was true "power"!

Why do I like traditional carols better than new holiday songs
Because they "ring-a-ling" with memories of the past.

I remember the days when you only got one holiday gift—
and you were grateful!

Why did the ornaments on the tree tell stories?
Because they were "heirlooms"—they've seen it all!

Riddles for the Wise

Welcome to "Riddles for the Wise," a collection that will spark your curiosity and keep your mind sharp, while also tickling your funny bone. These riddles are designed to be a delightful blend of holiday humor, nostalgia, and playful wit.

Whether you're sharing them with friends and family, or just enjoying a quiet moment of reflection, these riddles are perfect for bringing a little challenge and a lot of joy to your day. With themes ranging from holiday traditions to the quirks of growing older, these riddles are sure to make you smile and reminisce.

Let's see if you can solve them all—no peeking at the answers!

Family and Tradition Riddles

I'm made with dough, sugar, and love, often decorated
by little hands with gloves. What am I?
Holiday cookies!

Why do the grandchildren love me more at
family gatherings?
Because I bring cookies and gifts!

I'm always at the table during big family dinners,
but I'm never eaten, and I cause a lot of talk.
What am I?
Family drama!

What makes Grandma smile, has a special crunch,
and always leaves the little ones in a sticky mess?
Candy canes!

I come after dinner, and you may find me in the living room o
kitchen. I make everyone groan, but it's tradition.
What am I?
Dishwashing!

What do you bring out every year, but only
when the grandkids are near?
The photo albums!

Growing Older Riddles

I count down to a special day, but I'm not a clock. I help you remember, even if your memory's in shock. What am I?

An advent calendar!

I'm something you need more of as you age, but I always disappear quickly during family gatherings.
What am I?

Patience!

I'm a gift that's given from the heart, and I often come in the form of baked tarts. What am I?

A homemade present!

I come in handy on family celebration days, especially for Grandpa, after too much turkey and play.
What am I?

A recliner chair!

What am I if I make you remember things from long ago, and every year I get more valuable as you grow?

Memories!

creak more as I get older, but I still bring joy when you give me a gentle push. What am I?

A rocking chair!

Why do seniors and lights get along so well?
We both shine brightest with a little extra support!

Growing Older Riddles

I've seen many celebrations come and go, and I'm always found above the fire. What am I?

The mantel with old family photos!

What goes down every year, but your love for family only goes up?

The decorations after the holidays!

I'm something that gets louder with age and comes out more during family games. What am I?

Laughter!

What am I if I always help you remember where you put things, even if I don't remember it myself?

A note on the fridge!

I used to be for playing outside, but now I'm more for keeping balance. What am I?

A cane!

What gets heavier the longer you hold it, but you still carry it everywhere you go?

Family love!

What takes more time as you age, but always feels like a cherished tradition at the end of the day?

Getting ready for bed!

Nostalgic Riddles

I'm something that's best when shared and even better when told over and over again. What am I?
A family story!

What comes with years and never stops growing, even though you can't see it?
Wisdom!

I come in handy during conversations, especially when recalling something from the past. What am I?
A good pair of glasses!

Why does age bring more laughter to games?
Because we've learned not to take winning or losing too seriously!

I am something you used to have to wind up, and I played your favorite songs with a clunk and a thump. What am I?
A music box!

I'm a toy without batteries that kept everyone entertained, and you had to wind me up again and again. What am I?
A jack-in-the-box!

One-Liners for Golden Giggles

Welcome to "One-Liners for Golden Giggles," a collection of quick, witty jokes designed to make you smile, chuckle, and maybe even nod along in agreement. These one-liners are perfect for sharing with friends, entertaining family, or just enjoying yourself.

We've mixed nostalgia, family humor, and the perks (and quirks) of growing older into these jokes, keeping them lighthearted, relatable, and memorable.

Whether it's poking fun at grandkids, laughing at the joys of aging, or reminiscing about the good old days, these one-liners are here to deliver a dash of humor with every line.

Get ready to laugh out loud!

One-Liners for Golden Giggles

I love my grandkids, especially when they help me
remember where I put my glasses.

Grandkids are great—they're the reason I always
have cookies in the house.

I told my grandkids I was around before the internet
they asked if dinosaurs were too.

The grandkids wanted Wi-Fi—I gave them a
book and told them it's called "offline entertainment."

Grandkids: nature's way of making sure old people
don't get too much rest.

I let my grandkids win at hide-and-seek
—mostly because I forgot where I hid.

The best thing about grandkids?
They're like a boomerang—
they always come back for more treats.

I told my grandkids bedtime stories
I think they liked them because I fell asleep first.

Nostalgia and the Good Old Days

Back in my day, "streaming" was something
you did at the local creek.

We didn't need filters—our childhood photos were
blurry all on their own.

Remember when the only "screen time" was a window?
Yeah, that's why we played outside.

My first phone was attached to the wall… and it had a cord
that worked as a jump rope.

Remember when our playlists were on the radio, and the DJ
decided what came next?

They say age is just a number—mine's unlisted.

Getting older is like climbing a hill—you just keep
hoping there's a nice bench at the top.

Wrinkles are just proof that I smiled more than I frowned.

My body says I'm old, but my heart says,
"Let's dance" … my knees disagree.

Nostalgia and the Good Old Days

At my age, "getting lucky" means
remembering where I parked the car.

The holidays are great—it's the only time of year
I get away with napping at every party.

Decorating for the holidays takes hours
taking it all down takes until June.

My holiday plan is simple: eat, nap, repeat.

Mistletoe used to mean kisses
now it's a good excuse for some peace and quiet.

I asked the grandkids to help me decorate
they used enough glitter to make my vacuum retire.

My favorite part of holiday dinners is telling
the same story and pretending it's the first time.

Holidays: when your family visits to remind you
why you enjoy the quiet.

The secret to surviving holiday gatherings?
Sit near the desserts and smile.

Holiday Tales with a Touch of Nostalgia

The holiday season is a perfect time to reflect, laugh, and enjoy the small surprises that life brings. These stories are crafted for those who have seen countless Christmases come and go, each one filled with its share of surprises and hiccups.

Let's share some laughter, as these tales remind us of the holiday magic that never truly gets old.

The Bingo Blowout

Marge and her friends had been attending their weekly bingo game for as long as anyone could remember. The community center had decided to spice things up for the holidays, announcing a "Holiday Bingo Blowout" with Christmas-themed prizes and, supposedly, a special surprise guest. Marge was thrilled. She figured the special guest might be someone like Santa, which, at this age, would at least mean getting a few candy canes.

When they arrived, the decorations were already in full swing—tinsel hanging from the ceiling, candy canes at every table, and enough holiday music to make you dizzy. Marge took her usual seat with her best friends, Gladys and Harold.

The game began like any other, except the prizes were strange. Gladys won the first round and received a giant fruitcake wrapped in cellophane, the kind nobody really wants but pretends to enjoy.

"Well, at least you can use it as a doorstop," Harold quipped, nudging Gladys.

Gladys rolled her eyes. "Maybe I'll gift it back to Edna next year. She'd never know!"

The highlight of the evening came when the "special guest" was revealed. Marge was ready for a man in a Santa suit. Instead, it was Edna—the overly enthusiastic activities coordinator—dressed as a Christmas elf. Edna bounded to the front, waving a tambourine and singing "Jingle Bells" off-key.

The room fell silent for a moment before Harold, never one to hold back, leaned over to Marge and whispered loudly enough for everyone to hear, "I was hoping for Frank Sinatra, but I guess we got his opening act!"

The whole room erupted in laughter. Even Edna had to pause and chuckle before finishing her song. Though it wasn't exactly the magical surprise Marge had expected, she couldn't help but enjoy every second of the chaos.

They might not have gotten a real Santa, but they did leave with smiles—and a fruitcake they all vowed to re-gift.

As Marge left, she turned to Harold, still chuckling. "You know, sometimes it's the unexpected that makes these nights worth it."

Harold nodded. "Especially when it involves fruitcake and an elf tambourine."

The Great Cookie Mix-Up

Helen was known throughout the neighborhood for her Christmas cookies. Every December, she baked dozens upon dozens of gingerbread men, sugar cookies, and her famous chocolate chip delights. This year, she was feeling adventurous and decided to try a new recipe she found online—a batch of "holiday spice" cookies. The description promised warmth, a bit of spice, and just the right hint of nostalgia.

Helen followed the recipe exactly—or so she thought. The dough looked a little different, but she figured it was just because of the extra spices. She baked them, decorated them with red and green icing, and packed them into tins for her friends at the senior center. When she arrived, everyone was delighted to see her coming with her famous cookies.

"Look who's here! Helen with the best cookies in town!" George exclaimed, rubbing his hands together eagerly.

Helen smiled. "Don't get too excited, George. I tried something new this year."

The first person to take a bite was George, who had been eyeing the cookies since Helen walked in. He took a big bite, paused, and then immediately began coughing. "Helen, did you add pepper to these?" he sputtered, tears welling up in his eyes.

Helen quickly took a bite herself—and realized her mistake. Instead of grabbing cinnamon, she had used cayenne pepper, making her "holiday spice" cookies taste more like a practical joke. Her eyes widened, and then she burst out laughing.

"Oh dear, I think I've invented the first-ever Christmas cookie that fights back!" Helen said, giggling.

The room burst into laughter as Helen, blushing but amused, apologized. "Well, I guess they'll warm you up in this cold weather!" she said, chuckling along with the group. From that day on, George insisted that Helen make her "spicy surprise" cookies every year, just for the laughs.

And Helen, ever the good sport, promised to label her spices more clearly—but secretly loved the story that her accidental "pepper cookies" gave them all.

"And George," Helen added with a wink, "next year, I'll add an extra dash just for you!"

The Christmas Tree Fiasco

Frank and Mildred had been married for over fifty years, and each Christmas, Frank insisted on getting the biggest, best Christmas tree he could find. It was tradition—though Mildred would always remind him that "biggest" wasn't always "best," especially when it came to maneuvering it into their small living room.

This year, Frank found a tree that was practically perfect. It was tall, full, and just the right shade of green. The only problem? It was also a foot taller than their ceiling. But Frank, being resourceful, wasn't going to let that stop him. He decided that if he just trimmed a bit off the top, it would fit perfectly. Mildred watched, sipping her tea, as Frank brought the tree inside and attempted his modifications.

The problem arose when Frank's "trimming" took a little too much off the top, resulting in a lopsided tree that now looked like it had a severe flat-top haircut. Mildred tried to stifle her giggles, but it was no use.

"Frank, I think we've got the only Christmas tree that needs a hat," she said, trying to hold back her laughter.

Undeterred, Frank had an idea. He went to the closet, pulled out one of his old fishing hats, and placed it right on top of the tree. "There! Problem solved," he said, grinning from ear to ear.

Mildred shook her head, still laughing. "You know, Frank, sometimes I think you do these things just to keep me entertained."

Frank gave her a wink. "Well, as long as it makes you smile, I figure I'm doing something right."

By the time their grandchildren arrived to visit, the tree had become the centerpiece of the holiday—a perfectly imperfect tree wearing Grandpa's fishing hat. The children laughed and insisted on hanging ornaments all around the hat, adding to its charm.

And as they gathered around to decorate it, Mildred knew that this, too, would become one of those family stories they'd tell every Christmas—a reminder that sometimes the best decorations are the memories you make along the way.

Until We Meet Again, Ho-Ho-Hilariously!

Well, here we are at the end of our laugh-filled sleigh ride! You've cruised through puns, tackled reindeer riddles, and chuckled at one-liners.

You've giggled, groaned (the good kind!), and maybe even laughed so loud that someone had to ask, "What's so funny?!"

Before you slide this joke book back into a stocking or onto a shelf, remember: laughter is the best gift—it doesn't need wrapping, it's impossible to break, and there's no receipt needed! Whether you were reading aloud by the glow of a twinkling Christmas tree, in a car packed with family, or simply enjoying some quiet giggles, I hope these jokes brought you closer to those you love.

Now that you've got a pocket full of holiday humor, use it wisely. Pull out a joke whenever Uncle Jerry starts his long-winded stories, or when the holiday dinner gets a little too serious.

Share them, tweak them, and make your own—because laughter is a gift that keeps on giving.

Thanks for joining this merry, joke-filled adventure. May your holidays always be full of warmth, cheer, and enough humor to make even Santa crack a smile.

Until next time, keep those giggles jingling!

P.S. If you loved these jokes, share the joy—because a day without laughter is like a sleigh without reindeer: it just doesn't fly!

Loved the Book? Let Us Know!

Hey there!

If you enjoyed the book, we'd love to hear what you think! It only takes about **30 seconds**, and your review would really help us out (seriously, quicker than Santa can finish a Christmas cookie!).

Just **scan the QR code**—it's similar to the process you used to **claim your extras**, but this time it will take you straight to Amazon to leave a **star rating or full review**.

Every bit of feedback helps others discover the book, and we'd truly **appreciate** it.

Thanks!

48624761R00059